THE DIGITAL MARKETING SUCCESS FORMULA

6 SIMPLE STEPS TO ATTRACT AND RETAIN
THE PERFECT CLIENT ONLINE

THE DIGITAL MARKETING SUCCESS FORMULA

6 SIMPLE STEPS TO ATTRACT AND RETAIN
THE PERFECT CLIENT ONLINE

Heather J. Crider

Copyright © 2017 by Heather J. Crider
All rights reserved. No part of this book may be reproduced, scanned,
or distributed in any printed or electronic form without permission.
First Edition: 2017
Printed in the United States of America
ISBN: 978-1-947289-88-8

To Joyce, Jim, and Samantha, who have all inspired me never to give up and live each day to its fullest, no matter what comes my way.

It is when we forget all our learning that we begin to know.
> –Henry David Thoreau

Until you start believing in yourself, you ain't gonna have a life.
> –Rocky Balboa

When you're going through Hell, keep going.
> –Winston Churchill

You have enemies? Good. That means you've stood up for something, sometime in your life.
> –Winston Churchill

When you reach the end of your rope, tie a knot in it and hang on.
> –Franklin D. Roosevelt

TABLE OF CONTENTS

Introduction to Digital Marketing	1
Common Mistakes	8
Keeping It Real	20
The Formula	24
Phase One: Attract	26
Phase Two: Engage	42
Phase Three: Capture	49
Phase Four: Convert	61
Phase Five: Retain	72
Phase Six: Repeat	79
Where To Start	98
Email Marketing	102
Content Marketing	110
Six Essential Components To Create Attractive Viral-Worthy Content	117
Getting Traffic	119
Video Marketing Strategy	136
PPC	139
Advanced Methods	143

The Digital Marketing Success Formula

~Preface~

Over the past twenty years of being in business, I've learned a lot of bad habits: mainly to be stressed, to work until exhaustion, and always to be closing. Don't get me wrong, those habits have good uses at times, and have many times for me, but they also lead to burnout and frustration. Usually small-business owners and entrepreneurs loathe marketing and selling. They just want to do what they are good at.

When I first decided to write this book, it was purely out of frustration over the online and marketing worlds. There are many wonderful books that seek to add value and give one or two nuggets of information, and most do accomplish this task. The problem I kept hearing from business owners was they didn't know how to apply all the information or how to make it work for them.

Once I took a step back and really studied what worked both for me when my businesses were the most successful, and for the successful businesses I have assisted over the past 14 years, I realized there was a formula, even if we didn't realize we were following the formula.

The Success Formula was then created. I began to break down each of the six steps and the phases within each step. My clients and students then started to have a clearer understanding of what they were doing and why. They began to simplify what they did and implement simpler processes in which they could get more clients without over-stressing and reducing the amount of time it usually took to get more clients.

Naturally, my own business began to experience exponential growth when I too realized the simplicity of the Success Formula as well as the processes inside of each step.

This book explains the Success Formula and each of the six steps. It goes into detail on each step and how to apply the steps in your business. It also summarizes the main marketing strategies and why I feel that you must master two essential strategies first before employing any other strategy.

As you progress through this book and each step and phase, you will actually be building a roadmap. The Success Formula will become your compass while implementing your marketing plan in each phase.

Let me explain briefly why I chose to call this a Success Formula. Besides the fact that I came from an accounting background where I solved complex business decisions using formulae, I believe when we understand a formula, our brains can repeat the process and become more comfortable moving forward. I've been in business way too long to believe stress never exists. However, I also have been around the Sun enough times now to have learned how powerful our minds are and the impact stress has on our overall success and fulfillment. Therefore, if we can follow a formula and have the confidence and certainty that the formula works, then our minds will automatically become more certain, relaxed, and less stressed.

I urge you to remain patient throughout the phases and the processes. Most of us tend to want to jump straight into the creation and implementation phases. I've done it myself and it usually cost me more time and money in the long run. If you can understand the phases and the processes, and remain patient, then when you do implement, it will be simpler and clearer.

My goal in writing this book is to provide such certainty and perhaps a compass so business owners and entrepreneurs can walk the path knowing they can achieve success with their digital marketing.

Another goal is to help business owners and entrepreneurs understand that professional success can lead to so much more. We can't give what we don't have, and the more successful we can become, the more of an impact we can make on the whole world. Making a large impact and doing great things in the world is truly my ultimate goal. Since this book focuses on the principles and Success Formula for digital marketing, I want every business owner to fulfill their dreams, become better people, and make a large impact on the world.

To be honest, after writing this book, I realized it was more for me than anyone else. Wow, that really sounds selfish to say out loud! However, the realization I came to while writing this book is that this stuff really does work. It is truly a simplified formula that, if followed and applied, can have a big impact. I needed to reconnect these principles to my own brain to understand that what I have been doing and helping others do to succeed works, and works very well.

My hope for you is that you have massive success, less stress, a ton more fun, a life of incredible abundance, and fulfillment, so you can make an enormous impact and create your legacy.

My life certainly has not been perfect, but I have been truly blessed and fortunate with periods of success. I have had wonderful experiences in a corporate career followed by true independence in my own businesses. I have not had a traditional 'job' now for over 14 years. What an incredible accomplishment in this world today to be truly free from a clock and not having to ask for time off to attend my children's events and do the things I want to do. I mean no disrespect to those who are still in the "9 to 5" world. I have been able not only to survive, but also thrive.

When I say periods of success, I have also been blessed to have had a life full of failure and struggle. These struggles have taught me how to appreciate the simple things and also the people who come in and out of my life, and those who have remained in my life. Both my successes and failures have allowed me to experience first-hand what works and what does not. It has allowed me to share with others so you can shorten your own learning curve and lessen the stress of growing and scaling a business.

My true goal and purpose is to help others succeed and have extraordinary fulfillment. I believe we can have it all if we simplify our minds and learn the art of mindfulness and appreciation. Asking for "it all" is not selfish or out of reach. The only limitations we have are those we place on ourselves, and what an ultimate act of selfishness that is, not to share with the world.

Preface

I would like to thank anyone who has ever had an impact on my life, positive or otherwise. If it weren't for all my experiences, I would not be who I am today and I am truly grateful for you all.

Thank you so much to my children, Audrey and Sawyer, for choosing me to be your Mommy and for being the inspiring little people in my life who push me daily. I wish for you to be proud of me knowing you too can have the life of your dreams, if you do the work to achieve it and always believe.

Thank you to Dr. Gabriel Grabarek, who provided me with an incredible amount of love, encouragement, and support during the process of reading and commenting on my work. I am not sure I could have even published this without your help and guidance. Thank you for being an incredible part of my life.

Thank you to my closest friends and family who have loved me despite my flaws. There are too many wonderful people to list by name, just know you all are so very important to me. You have loved me unconditionally while pushing me to be a better version of myself. Thank you for also providing the well needed kick in the pants when I needed it.

Thank you for those who have had belief in me, when at times I did not believe in myself, and for telling me repeatedly, that if anyone can do it, I can.

Finally, thank you to all my teachers and mentors, some of whom I've never even met personally. All your works and dedication to spreading your message to the world is inspiring and truly making a difference. I hope to do the same.

To Download An Action Guide To Follow Along With This Book - Head Over To
www.heatherjcrider.com/success-path

or

email

admin@heatherjcrider.com

The Digital Marketing Success Formula

Introduction to Digital Marketing

Digital Marketing. Ick! What? What does digital marketing even mean? Digital marketing means getting your business noticed online to increase sales and profits. Or stated differently, anything you do online to drive people to you. Period. It's that simple.

You're thinking, "Yeah, right. Not so simple." In fact, the thought of digital marketing can be downright nauseating sometimes, can't it?

Picture the following setting with me for a moment. You're with your favorite people enjoying a beautiful afternoon basking in the sun feeling the warm sunshine on your face as the hot, soft sand squishes between your toes while you listen to the waves of the ocean crash along the shoreline.

You take a quick break to check your smart phone while you sip on your favorite drink and you see dozens of notifications for new sales, new customers, and tons of new traffic to your website.

That's the moment you realize all your hard work and digital marketing efforts are paying off for you and your business. You realize it is allowing you the time, money, and freedom to enjoy these precious moments.

How great would it be to enjoy a vacation relaxing while your business is still working for you even though you are taking a much-needed break rejuvenating yourself? That's the ultimate goal of business, isn't it? To make a profit and enjoy life.

The ultimate goal of digital marketing is to have all the processes in place to automate your business and still grow it at the same time. My belief is that no matter what your business is, you can create recurring revenue through automation efforts. The technology is here, so why not use it.

I also believe it doesn't have to become too complicated, which is why I decided to develop this formula. There were years of struggling and a lot of sleepless nights that I went through to understand this whole "making a profit online" thing. Although tactics and technology do change rapidly each year, the overall strategy and basics don't really change all that much. My goal when I finally decided to put this book together was to simplify the process and the learning curve. I want other entrepreneurs and business owners to realize that digital marketing does not have to be as overwhelming as it seems.

My goal is to empower as many people as I can with a few simple strategies that could change the course of their businesses, which would then impact their entire life. We are in a time right now, because of technology, where being a business owner and entrepreneur couldn't be easier. However, so many people give up just before they succeed, because they are overwhelmed. When I'm coaching and working with clients, I tend to cite example after example and, quite frankly, talk way too much. I've tamed myself in this book to keep things simple. The formula in this book will not only reduce the overwhelmed feeling, but also give you hope and encouragement to exponentially grow your business.

The Success Formula all entrepreneurs and business owners must master also includes mastering our own emotions. This can be hard to really accomplish, as we are emotional beings pouring our hearts and souls into our businesses. The key here is to remember how to manage becoming a success and taking care of yourself.

Most people believe that digital marketing can make you an overnight success. However, most of us aren't lucky enough to create that ONE post or article that just gets the internet buzzing, causing thousands of excited visitors to land on your site and become enthusiastic customers clamoring to buy from you immediately. Although you think you know similar stories, they usually don't happen exactly like this.

Digital Marketing is simply anything you do online to get attention and traffic to you or your business.

You can be an overwhelming success with some strategy and deliberate action, as long as it's the right action. Digital marketing is a process. It's the formation of specific strategies, implementing those strategies, and the creation of consistent processes attracting the right traffic (customers) to your website. The more traffic you receive (readers, subscribers, etc.) the more opportunity you have to convert them into paying customers. Thus, more sales and profits for you and your business.

In This Guide We Will Cover...

- Common mistakes and how to avoid them
- The importance of understanding strategy
- How to plan in each phase
- The Digital Marketing Formula
- How to become a mind reader by researching the main problems your audience is facing
- Narrowing down the one or two goals in YOUR marketing plan

- Engaging your audience by speaking their language and offering value
- Going where your audience is and going after the offer
- The magic of messaging
- Converting your audience by creating an "Oh Yes!" offer
- Creating a retention strategy that will work for you to create a loyal base of repeat-buying customers
- Reflecting and analyzing what works and what doesn't
- The importance of an email marketing campaign
- How to create attractive viral-worthy content
- How to manage and use social media
- The value of video marketing
- PPC Overview
- Growing with the funnel
- Advanced techniques and search engine marketing overview

Introduction

Common Mistakes

Why is it so important to understand the "Do Not's" before the "Do's"?

Simple.

I want you to know how to save yourself from wasting your valuable time and money. There are a lot, and I mean A LOT, of theories out there about marketing and digital marketing. There are some great experts and some people claiming to be experts. At the end of the day, I want to save you from potentially losing thousands of hours and dollars. And I want you to succeed.

I'll save you from the headache and the endless trial and error phases. If I showed you all the money I've spent on various courses, tests, businesses, and experiments I've done over the years, your head would spin! Mine is spinning again now just thinking about all the uphill battles I've faced (and, of course, conquered).

I've been an entrepreneur now for over fourteen years. When I started my first real corporation, I was in my mid-twenties and thought I knew everything. Technically, I've been an entrepreneur ever since I was five and started a clothes-ironing business in my front yard. It wasn't very profitable. In fact, not at all.

Believe it or not, as a five-year-old I began to understand the importance of what people want, rather than what they need. How crazy is it that a five-year-old would even think about ironing clothes for a business?

Most of the businesses I've started were very successful, although that one did fail. The reason I've been able to succeed was always because of sound strategy and understanding the message. For me, over the years the message has remained clear: grow your marketing efforts in the most strategic and efficient manner possible.

This is what I want to show you: what works, so you can get to it and grow your business. But first, as I said earlier, let's cover the "Do Not's".

Most Common Mistakes People Make in Digital Marketing.

Common Mistake #1. Dabble in marketing using everyone's "advice."

Does this sound familiar:

"We've tried every technique you can think of, and nothing seems to work. We've followed everything the experts keep saying and even the advice we've heard from other businesses we know. But it becomes too overwhelming and just doesn't work for us"

Can you relate to this statement at all? Becoming overwhelmed can happen so fast in all marketing, especially when so many different experts are telling you about different methods. This sounds like a simple mistake, but it's actually rather complicated.

I call this the water cooler discussion error since everyone has an opinion at the water cooler. Do you remember during your 9-5 job, in corporate America, at gatherings or events, when you would take breaks and hang out by the coffee machine, or snack room, or wherever else? Conversations would get going about how things were going and what frustrations you were having. Before you knew it, you were getting advice from everyone and suddenly everyone was an expert. Someone would talk about this one experience they told you to try, or heard about a cousin that put up one blog post and instantly became a millionaire, or any number of other 'expert' opinions. These coworkers of yours likely had really good intentions to help you. They truly thought that this short conversation might just in fact change your life. But, this was so often such a quick glance at your situation without any real authority or understanding.

What I mean is, just because your cousin's sister in-law's nephew learned in his computer class that you should blog every Tuesday at one a.m. and create your website on Drupal, doesn't mean that that's the best approach for you. Or even better, Expert X says SEO is the best and only method to get traffic, while Expert Y says PPC is the absolute best method, then Expert Z says the only possible way to get traffic to your site is social media methods. I'm not saying these people don't care about you, because they likely do, but some gurus are manipulating you and creating an urgency for you to do it their way or else you are doomed to failure. These experts have belief in their own methods and their methods are all correct.

But are they correct for you?

Is your strategy in place to implement their method? Do you have a strategy? Do you have too many strategies? Do you even understand their method? Are you trying all the methods? There are so many methods and gurus that it can be very confusing.

"Thank you for gently guiding me toward insight."

Now, I may be a little harsh with that analogy, but you get the picture. Sure, there's great advice out there, and a lot of wonderful gurus and experts do exist with wonderful advice. Some does and will work for you. But not all will work for you, not without a consistent process and plan to know when to implement certain strategies within a plan that works for you and your business.

It can all be confusing, and it's all about timing. It's about picking the right time to implement a method for you, and then cutting out all the noise that does not support that method: following ONLY one strategy at a time.

My goal is to simplify the process for you and create less stress and confusion.

Common Mistake #2. Dabbling without commitment

Does this statement sound familiar?

"We are thinking of doing a targeted social media campaign but haven't gotten around to it because we don't really want to invest the time and energy without guaranteed results."

This may be more of an obvious statement, but I've seen more anxious business owners than I can count give up before they fully give a method a chance. They kind of try a method, then get frustrated. They give up and try another method without the proper sequences, measurements, certainty, and, most importantly, PATIENCE.

I've been there myself, too. In fact, I've been scared out of my mind in the past to really put forth a lot of effort and commitment into certain methods. There is a huge fear when it comes to trying new and different methods without the certainty that they are going to work, especially with newer businesses or business owners who are already spread so thin.

Patience is a tough one for business owners, too. It can be overwhelming for business owners to juggle all the roles and wear all the hats to get everything done. However, it's hard to thoroughly give a method a chance and properly test it to its fullest potential if you jump ship too quickly and aren't fully committed.

You want results, and you wanted them yesterday, I get that…loud and clear.

But being committed to your plan (assuming you have a plan!) is essential. My goal in this guide is to help simplify the process for you so you can fully commit to your marketing plan.

Common Mistake #3. Spending more time on management than marketing.

Warning: this one may sting a little!

How does this statement resonate with you?

"Most of our marketing budget is allocated to our golf sponsorships and calendars we pass out. We considered adding more to our marketing budget if we had more sales and customers, but right now we are focused on expansion."

WHAT???? You are trying to expand but don't dedicate your resources to marketing! Have you heard business owners saying anything similar? Again, I get it. As business owners we only have so much time to focus our efforts, but how can we get more sales and customers if we don't add new strategies to get them? (no offense to those who use golf sponsorships as your marketing, but that's not marketing, that's just community donations and outreach)

Now, this one, in my opinion, is the deadliest of mistakes. It's a two-fold problem. Before I expand upon this one, I would like for you to answer the following question: How much of your time, energy, and money are dedicated to the following areas in your business? (in terms of percentage in each of the following areas)

Production:

Operations:

Marketing:

Did you know most business owners get this one wrong?

Common Mistakes

Perhaps wrong is misguided. They aren't wrong, they're just misinformed. They also are just not committed and have a lack a full belief in their marketing to employ the right tactics to ensure marketing is #1.

MOST businesses will spend 35-40 % in Production, 35-40% in Operations, and 20-30% in Sales and Marketing.

The <u>most successful companies and businesses</u> break down their focus into the following business areas.

60% Marketing
20% Production
20% Operations

Does this sound doable? Scary? Out of line? Why are these numbers so different than the average company's numbers? Successful businesses understand the importance of sales and marketing. As business owners we need to create a traffic problem to a store before we can really worry about improvement of operations.

I usually ask clients what good is a fully functional and operational store (or website) in the middle of the forest, without a highway to get people to it or signs showing them that it exists? This is kind of like putting all our energy into 'creating' the perfect product, service or solution, but not showing our customers we exist.

Get people to start talking about you. Create customers, fans, and followers who cannot wait to get in line at your store, THEN deliver to them the perfect experience or product. (Think Kickstarter or CrowdSourcing models….)

Those numbers above do include all marketing, not just digital marketing. However, you can see in today's world that digital marketing is essential, and with the right plan and dedication, your business can grow ten to twenty times, and even more.

We will talk later on how to simplify your plan so that this does not sound quite so scary. These numbers are doable. And we'll help you get there.

The goal is focusing on a few key strategies that can take an unknown blog and turn it into a winning and profitable business.

Common Mistakes
Chapter Exercise:

Write below what two or three things you can to do to put more focus into sales and marketing?

Keeping It Real

Let's be honest here for a moment, shall we? I have to be realistic with my message. Will your business grow or double overnight? Maybe. Maybe not. Probably not. Will your followers grow to over a million? Maybe. Maybe not. Probably not. However, you don't have to have a large group of followers to be successful.

This guide is intended to help you attract and retain the perfect clients for you and your business. You don't have to have a million followers to double or triple your business. You just have to have the RIGHT type of paying customers who are attracted to you. I'll show you how to get started. If you want to grow to over a million followers, we'll help you get there too.

Not all businesses are the same. You will be in different stages at different times throughout the life of your business. There are very tactical strategies for each stage to see significant growth, but you have to know what stage you are in and what methods will work best for you. You also have to be open minded and willing to commit.

Just like the first day at the gym. If you've never been to a gym before, then chances are you'll be very nervous and intimidated by the equipment. You may even cut a workout short to have less risk of looking like you don't know what you're doing. It can be scary and maybe even overwhelming. But, you show up anyway.

However, if you are a veteran gym goer and then one day you stroll into new gym you will likely walk around a few times to see what equipment they have and then quickly develop a game plan in your mind of what equipment to use and what workout you'll accomplish that day, then you'll get started and stick around with confidence.

Remember though, the veteran gym rat was once the gym rookie.

The Digital Marketing Success Formula

The veteran gym rats were once intimidated as well, and it took a process of learning, trial and error, and experience to get to the gym rat level. Whether you are new, newer, or a veteran, there are clear goals and strategies that will help you grow along the way. Depending on your experience level, failures, and victories, you will approach things differently. This is the case in any business. The stage you are in and the experiences you have had will all impact the methods you will employ to help you get where you want to go.

Having said all of this, the process should be simple.

The process should not become over-complicated from all the noise, experts, and advertising you see every day. Remember, successful marketers are doing what they do best: marketing. So don't get caught in an overwhelming marketing vortex. Make a plan that works for you and your business. Cut out the noise and only listen to the things that honor your plan and focus at that moment.

Before we learn how to do this and dive into the actual processes, it's important to do some work up front to set yourself up for success.

If you fail to plan, you plan to fail. So PLAN.

Plan on spending some time understanding each of the phases in the following chapters. Do the exercises and give yourself enough time to really process and think about your business and where you are right now and where you want to go. Think about what is working and not working. Put a plan in place for each step or phase. I'll help you as much as I can in this process, but you have to show up and do some work as well!

The Formula

Six Simple Phases to Attract and Retain the Perfect Client and to Master Your Business Marketing Online

(broken down into phases because "phases" sounds better than "steps")

The Formula: Phase One

The Digital Marketing Success Formula
6 Simple Steps To Attract & Retain The Perfect Client

1. **ATTRACT** — Know your audience and their needs
2. **ENGAGE** — Communicate and Show Up/ Provide Content To Address Your Audience Needs
3. **CAPTURE** — Provide Incentive/Value In Exchange For Audience Information
4. **CONVERT** — Provide Irresistible OH YES Value To Convert To Paying Customer.
5. **RETAIN** — Treat Customers Like Royalty To Create Loyalty. Get THEM Talking About YOU.
6. **REPEAT** — Analyze What Worked Well and REPEAT

Heather J. Crider

www.heathercrider.com

Phase One: Attract

The Attraction Phase is making yourself attractive to your audience by UNDERSTANDING THEM. You want your client or customer to say to you, "How did you read my mind?" In this phase, you must understand your client's problems.

I would like to challenge you here to forget for a moment what you think you know about your clients. This phase is really essential to thoroughly understanding what your client/audience/customer wants.

Don't say that you already do. I promise that you don't, at least not as thoroughly as you could. Not, yet. This statement cannot be expressed clearly enough. In five of the six phases, knowing and understanding your client is vital to your success. When I say understanding them, what I mean is to know as much as you can about their issues and how much better their lives will be because of you and how you solved their problem. Knowing this will help you communicate more effectively. It will help you speak their language. It will help you convert them into paying customers in later phases. After all, that's the goal, right? You want to provide value and convert them into paying customers.

You are the provider of the product or service that solves a problem. This product or solution is solving their immediate and obvious external problem. Customers always have two sets of problems and don't really know it or express it in that way.

External - This is the obvious problem.

Internal - This is all the good stuff customers want to experience because their issues have been solved, or another way of saying it...

The internal problem is all the bad stuff your customers are currently experiencing because they don't have the solution... yet.

You must not only understand their obvious external problems, but it is also crucial for you to understand their internal problems. In fact, you have to know them better than they know themselves. These problems may seem obvious, but usually are much deeper than what they say or are presenting. Remember that the product or service you are offering is only part of the solution. What is really being offered is altering their state of mind. Your product or service is taking them from a place (fear, doubt, frustration, confusion, worry, lack of knowledge or understanding, etc.) and moving them into a place where they want to be or become (content, relief, happiness, fulfillment, satisfaction, etc.).

These internal problems are the things blocking them, preventing them, or holding them back. These problems are the voices in their heads.

And no matter how big or small these internal voices are, they are all important.

The problems are also people getting in their own way. They are all the concerns, doubts, frustrations, limitations, and misunderstandings they are experiencing. YOU have the solution. The solution is always so much more than a product or service. It's the happy place. A new found attitude. The relief. The transformation. The solution you are offering provides the mechanism to move them into a peace of mind that is transformational.

No matter how big or small a problem seems, having it solved moves someone from a state of unhappiness to, at the very least, a state of contentment. That very state of being needs to be your focus.

Have you ever had a conversation with someone and they kept answering your questions in the form of questions? Their questions seemed as if they've experienced the same thing, and you left the conversation thinking, "It's like they read my mind. They understood me and knew exactly what I was thinking."

THAT'S the kind of connection you want with your client/customer/prospect. You want them to believe you're a mind reader, that you really do get them. This will also set you apart and position you as an authority on the topic.

Why an authority? Because you understand and speak their language and connect to their problems.

BUT HOW?

How do I gain a better understanding of my audience? I already serve them and know all about them. How can I understand them even more?

Do the research.

Be open to learning more. Forget what you think you know. You may know a lot and you probably do know a lot. But forget it for a little bit and do some research. No matter what product or service, I promise this will help you. It will help enhance what you are already offering. It will help you connect better. It will help you later with forming new messaging and connections.

First – Start with the end in mind. What is the solution you have? What is the problem it solves?

The Formula: Phase One

What are your customer's main concerns regarding this problem? What are all the internal conversations taking place inside of their heads?

Example -

Let's say you offer an organic health-food drink specifically for kids. This is a broad market, but a pretty good one to research. The solution is an organic and healthy diet for kids. There are lots of ways you can market this solution, just as there are many different types of problems you could solve.

Let's look at one problem to get a better understanding. The customer is the parent trying to get his or her children to eat healthier. Even though the product is for the child, the parent is the one buying the product and the one influencing the child.

The external problem: Picky kids not getting enough nutrition

The internal problem:
-I really want my child to be as healthy as possible.

-I want my child to have food that will not only help him grow but is also free from preservatives.
-I want my child to understand how good food affects his body.
-I know good food is essential for my child.
-I want to provide my child with the best food choices available.
-I've read enough and understand that processed food is bad for my child, but how do I get them to eat healthily?
-My child is suffering because of his lack of nutrition.
-My child is not doing well in school because he's not getting enough to eat and the right things to eat.
-My child is failing because of his lack of nutrition.
-I am a bad parent because I am not providing my child with the right kinds of foods.
-My child will develop diseases and conditions because of his lack of nutrition.
-My child will fail school and drop out because of his lack of nutrition, and it will be my fault.
-My child will live in my basement forever and be a menace to society because I was not able to give him the proper nutrition.

If you've ever been around picky kids who will only eat cheese puffs and hot dogs, then you know a little about this. (Is my child the only one who refuses to eat anything except cheese puffs and hot dogs?!)

Do you see the pattern here?

This parent's problem is providing a healthy food option for her child, but the internal dialogue (fears, doubts, frustrations, and concerns) are all equally as real. These internal dialogues and conversations are preventing her from feeling satisfied with a solution. Her pain is real to her and she desires not only a solution but desires to get rid of her 'internal problems' and pain. No matter how ridiculous a fear sounds or an internal problem sounds, it is very real for that parent. Most parents don't really believe their children will live in their basement forever because of a lack of nutrition when they are five, but crazier thoughts have occurred, so you must think of any and all concerns.

Remember, you want to be a mind reader. Get inside the minds of the parents who have the problem so you can position yourself as understanding and attract them to you as the authority on that topic to solve their problem. Knowing as many of these internal conversations and pain points, otherwise referred to as triggers, will help you communicate, write messaging, and present offers that will attract them to you and give you more of an opportunity to help them.

"But, I know my solution and the basic problem it solves for my client How do I understand more about them to identify with their internal struggles?"

Go to where they are and ask questions and LISTEN. There are many ways to show up and learn about your prospective customers. But to do so, you must consider yourself a bit of a spy and go where they go. There are a variety of places and methods: groups, face to face, your own client-group questionnaires, Google search, Amazon reviews, articles, Yelp reviews, Podcast interviews, Slack channels, Q&A sites, Quora, Slack, etc., to name a few.

If you have some sort of audience right now, go poll them. Create many different polls to find out what they are thinking. Rephrase questions in different ways to discover different responses. Go where they hang out. What groups are they members of? Join the groups, ask the questions, get involved. Go physically to where they are located, if you can. Read the same magazines, books, websites, etc., that will give you a better idea of the common branding and messaging and what they are being attracted to. Go to forums and see what conversations are taking place. There are many forums to which members belong and discuss the topics.

If you type in Google...Solution + Forum. This is where you can do a Google search of the other forums that exist and see what conversations are taking place.

> Q how to get my child to eat healthier forum
>
> Q how to get my child to eat healthier forum - Google Search

Facebook groups are quickly replacing a lot of these forums. Join the Facebook groups. Ask questions but also be that researcher looking to collect as much research as possible.

What to ask:

What do you think will happen if you don't do XYZ?

What kinds of things cause you to need XYZ? What is holding you back from exploring XYZ?

What are the reactions of your friends, family, colleagues, peers, if you obtain ABC? If you don't?

What really gets you fired up about XYZ?

What are the main benefits you would like to see if you have XYZ?

What would life be like if you could get your hands on ABC?

If you could sit with the expert in XYZ for one hour and ask any one question, what would it be?

What in your life at the moment is preventing you from seeking help with XYZ?

You get the picture. Ask questions about the problem and the solution, but mainly about the dialogue taking place inside of their heads to really get through to understand what they are experiencing right now.

What if you don't have your own audience, clients, or groups? Most of the 'spy tactics' described above don't involve you having your own group. You can research without a list. You can go to usertesting.com and collect paid data there. However, if you want your own group to research, then form a beta group, a research group, or a founding members group to start to collect data. Ask participants to help you by being a beta member. Tell them you have an amazing product and would like a few participants to help beta test. If they would join for free or a drastically reduced price, would they become a member and give their honest feedback as a case study. You can test them and see what they are talking about. A beta group is used in many stages of business, but it's also good to implement a Beta if you already have your product. It will give you more of a personal view. You still need a basic understanding of the problems they are facing to ask the right people to join.

Keep an ongoing market attraction and keyword research journal. Evernote is a great tool to use and keep track of your notes. I like it because it syncs to all your devices. Keep a 'marketing problem research' journal. Anytime you hear someone mention a problem or fear, or desire or need, this is gold for you to note. It will be used later, but will also help you understand them better anytime you communicate with them.

Your messaging depends on your research. Your messaging will become the key in future phases.

Attract Phase Action Exercise:

Write below:

What is the solution your product or services provide? (This is the answer to the external problem your audience is currently facing.)

Where can you go to ask questions of your audience?

What are the internal problems your audience is facing? What are the conversations taking place?

What are their main fears, frustrations, pain points and triggers?

Where would they like to be, or how would they like to feel once they've experienced your product or service?

Phase Two: Engage

The Engagement Phase is designed to create relevant conversations and develop information useful to your audience.

Now that you are inside the heads of your prospective customers and know their external and internal problems, you will need to know their immediate mindset and what they really want.
Most evenings when my family is having dinner, and I try to talk with my kids, I end up in some

philosophical rant about something that is meaningful only to me, but I'm trying to impress it upon my kids. Only, I find them staring at me wishing I would just stick pencils in their eyes. They don't care. They only care about what they care about.

It can be a little easier with kids to understand they only have an interest in what's important to them. However, this applies to your audience as well. Sure, there are some things you can share with them that may not be 100% relevant to their core issues, but ALWAYS come back to the conversation, material, offering, etc., in a way that IS relevant to them and has a correlation to their core issues.

When I was managing my wealth management agency and was still fairly new, I was so excited about sharing all my knowledge and information on how to save, invest, and manage wealth portfolios. I would prepare for my client meetings as if I were taking the SAT. I could not wait for them to come into my office so I could teach them everything I knew about investments.

They did come into my office. I did impress upon them some knowledge about their portfolio holdings, but also I became overly zealous about relaying the history of investments, patterns, predictions, statistics, and all the information I could think of that might be of slight interest. I did this because I was the one with the interest in the details, not them. They only cared about what they cared about, which were their core problems. My intentions were really good. In fact, they were too good, because I failed to see the forest for the trees. Investments and wealth management was my service, but not really my role entirely and not 100% what they wanted to talk about.

This sounds a little counterproductive when you are a service provider, doesn't it? I thought each client cared about the intricacies of investments like I did, and they wanted to know as much of the details as I did. However, I learned the hard way that I was wrong. What I needed to do was slow down and really listen. My agenda and my understanding clouded my ability to meet them where they were… at that moment.

At that moment it was not all about the technicalities, but more about what I could provide that really took care of their core issues: their fears, doubts, frustrations, and uncertainties.

The Engagement Process is taking what you know about your customer and tailoring your message to attract and engage the right customers. In my examples above, both in relating to my children and to my past clients, I was more concerned about my agenda than engaging with their needs. My goal when engaging is to meet people where they are now, to be able to communicate in a way that matters to them. I most certainly know more about my service or product, but what I know doesn't mean anything if I cannot get my audience to know that I understand their needs and can relate to them.

How do you engage with an audience?

Now you can think about you! "Finally, I get to talk about myself instead of the audience!" Nope, that's not what I mean.

You need to do a little moon-walking here and make a plan before you jump completely into engaging. If you don't know exactly what your goal is, then engaging just becomes great conversations with no real action or movement. This will make more sense later, but the point is: what do you want? Where are you headed? Now is the time to really think about where you want to go and where you are now.

Pick ONE method at the beginning. The overwhelming nature of digital marketing gets real very quickly. Why? Have you looked at all the different digital marketing methods lately? There are endless methods and theories. Just start with ONE.

These foundational steps are SO crucial, which is why I'm talking about them now instead of diving into tactical applications right away. If you jump straight in to implementing too many methods or blindly implementing strategies, then they will likely fail for you. If you don't take the time to thoroughly prep and really think about your goals and what you are trying to accomplish, then you are just hoping things will click for you.

Remember when I mentioned earlier all the experts telling you that they have the best and only method and all the various things you can try? This isn't their fault because they believe their method is the best and they should. The problem comes when, as entrepreneurs, we get squirrel syndrome thinking that one particular tool or widget or method is THE thing you need most right now.

Thinking the next best thing is going to take your business to one million followers overnight. Looking for the magic bullet or newest shiny object. Trust me, it will all still be there for you when you and your business are ready. The main ingredient at first is to pick ONE method that you can master and then add others along the way.

Unless you are hiring an experienced digital marketing manager or agency to implement everything for you, doing all digital marketing methods at once will blow up and discourage you.

How do you pick a method?

The Formula: Phase Two

You must ask what you want. To determine how to engage with your audience, you must first ask yourself: What is YOUR goal?

> Gain more sales?
> Build a larger list?
> Increase your Facebook following?
> Get published as an author?
> Get a speaking gig?
> Become the next Anthony Robbins?
> Sell a your product?
> Gain shares?
> Promote another product or service?

> Once you are clear on your ONE goal, it will be much easier to implement your strategy to engage with your audience.

We will go over the details later, but the two foundational marketing methods I suggest for anyone to master first are:

> Build your email marketing campaign.

Build your content marketing campaign.

Once you have mastered these two methods, then move forward with mastering other marketing methods.

Engage Phase Action Exercise:

How are you currently engaging with your audience?

What is your ONE main goal right now?

Do you feel your main goal is being achieved by your engagement strategy?

Are you engaging with what your audience needs?

Phase Three: Capture

The Capture Phase is just as it sounds: capturing your audience and their basic information.

    This phase is all about getting their attention. Waving in a crowded room so they will notice you, not because you are the loudest or most obnoxious, but because you have a real solution to help them and are introducing yourself to them.

    When I mentioned my wealth management example earlier and that I was speaking the wrong message to my clients, I learned so much by failing. Those lessons really helped me understand that I needed to pay attention to what I was saying and to whom. Some audiences would love the detailed investment dissertation, but most don't.

The Engagement Process was taking what you know about your customer and tailoring your message to engage the right customers. The Capture Process expands on the right audience at the right time and triggers curiosity. You have to not only pick the right message but also make sure it's the right audience. You already know what they're thinking, and you know that your message will be about them, but before you attempt to capture your audience, you must ask yourself two very important questions.

Will they pay for the solution?

Are you in the right room with the right audience?

WHAT? More research? Yep! Sorry to say, but we are still in the foundational phases. This is crucial to your success and getting to your dreams.

I know this is where businesses really start getting impatient. This is where you want to just go and do what you do best. You want to provide for people and get to work. But you must keep the reigns on yourself a little longer because this groundwork will help you immensely later. In order for you to get what you want you must be patient to make sure you attract the right audiences. If you take the much needed time now to really do this hard work, then in the later phases your clients will be lined up at your doors asking how to work with you.

So ask, will your prospective customer pay for the solution? Remember in the Attraction Phase when we were learning how to spy on our customers? Go back to your research and simply see if there are similar programs or services like yours. Are people paying other people for something similar? Most people feel if there are other similar types of products or services then they don't have a chance of competing. It is a good thing to have competition. In most cases, competition means you have a paying audience. There are rare exceptions when your product or service is extremely unique and niched.

But, the overall message here is the same. Is there a paying audience?

One way to see if what you are offering has value to an audience is to view the traffic patterns on the search terms. Are people searching for the particular thing you are offering, and paying for the solution?

You can simply ask your audience what it means to them to have the solution and if they would pay for the solution. If they are not willing to pay you, then you're wasting your time and talking to the wrong people, or maybe offering the wrong thing.

At five years old, I was offering to iron clothing. I had a tiny toy clothes iron I was so proud of and would put to good use by offering to iron people's clothing for twenty-five cents per piece. I set up a little stand on my front porch and had a sign out front. But, as my neighbors drove by, they could care less about having their clothes ironed.

Sadly, I was offering the wrong service in my market (as if I had a market at the time). The market I was in front of would not and did not pay me.
I had two choices. I could change my service or product, or move to a different market, if one existed,

to offer my service. Although my short-lived dream of being a professional clothes ironer that afternoon when I was five was a big disappointment, believe it or not, it taught me a lot of valuable lessons as I got older and could analyze it more thoroughly.

What if you could find an audience who are all eager to get started and are looking right now for someone like you? People who ask others where they can find the answer and are ready to go? People who are just what you are looking for and can help? That's your goal when you are attracting and capturing: finding all the right people at the right time.

Have you heard the analogy about net fishing versus spear fishing?

Net fishing is when you cast a wide net, scoop up everything you can, then rummage through the net discarding what you don't want or need and picking the best fish, if there are any left.

Spearfishing is when you get to hunt for the right fish, target it, position yourself, then spear and capture that one fish.

You'll hear a lot of marketing experts talk about spear fishing. It's a very targeted approach to capturing exactly the fish/target you want. I don't disagree with them, I just look at it in a different way. In our digital marketing process, we look at things a little differently (if you haven't already noticed). We combine the net and spear fishing models into the speared net.

What I mean by this is, instead of casting a wide net and hoping you will have one good catch in it, what would it look like to you if you were to concentrate your efforts to the pool where the fish are together and you know they are just what you're looking for, offering just the food that they need? You are targeting a very specific group or audience and then spearing, instead of spearing just one. You cast a net with spears attached to get a larger audience than just one.

All the phases we have been talking about so far have been narrowing down your audience with your message and having you show up at the right place at the right time with the right message. This is what I mean by a speared net. Casting to the right audience at the right time.

Once you know you're talking to the right audience and speaking the right messages while

The Formula: Phase Three

engaging them and setting yourself up as the authority, now it's time to do some capturing.

Capturing is offering something of value to your audience in exchange for some of their information. You need to capture some information to take your engagement to the next level. It's like asking for a third of fourth date. You're moving the relationship along from just a casual meeting or two, to a more interesting relationship of curiosity and further discovery.

How to capture?

Peak curiosity enough for your prospective customers to provide you with their information. Your goal here is to get your prospective customers in your "funnel." Have you heard this term before? Most marketers refer to it as adding subscribers, or adding to your list. The funnel is strictly the stages you move them through to ultimately become a buying customer. It's the formula. More importantly, this phase is about building a relationship and bringing value to your audience.

The Capture is essentially your way of offering something of value to prospective customers in exchange for their name and email. Otherwise known as the HOOK. You offer a hook that has value. The call to action is to enter their information in exchange for the valuable thing you are offering.

Example of Value Hooks:
- EBooks
- White Papers
- PDF Download – How To
- Free Webinar
    - (usually can get a phone number for text reminders before the webinar)
- Videos

Although we did just talk about a few of the How To's, I would STRONGLY encourage you to go through this whole system before jumping into creating a hook. As entrepreneurs, we tend to get anxious and just want to create and do. I've jumped the gun more times than I can count without sitting and doing the work first. Take time to fully understand the process before jumping straight to creation. This phase really should be one of the longest phases. This is the phase where you are going back through the Attraction and Engaging, and then Capturing. You keep attracting the right audience, showing up where they are, speaking the right messages that resonate with the state they currently are in and then you offer them some 'free' solution to help them.

FREE? But, I want to make money. I know you do. That's the ultimate goal. But, if you cannot get your audience to trust you and to connect with you, then they won't buy from you. Your goal here is to get them lined up outside of your door. Offer these value hooks in such a way that they want more. Give them the steps they need to follow to gain access to your product or solution, but create a demand for more. Engage with them by offering more value. Always keep the audience in mind and the messages they have been conveying to you when you do your research.

Before you can really go much further, now is the time to organize it all and create the process, if you haven't already. Why are we digging into the process so much? Because all business success comes from developing a clear and concise system. We didn't jump straight into the detail of the tactical applications because we need to clearly understand where we are going and accurately set the foundation.

It's also because digital marketing is so vast and can be overwhelming. It's imperative to clearly identify with your market so you become consistent with your messaging. Have you ever heard of copywriters? Copywriters are invaluable in digital marketing. Why? Because the messaging is what attracts, engages, captures, and ultimately converts a customer.

The Magic Is In The Messaging.

The messages you are researching and collecting will become your key phrases. You'll understand this more in a later phase, but just know speaking the right message can really help to attract your audience. The whole goal with any marketing effort is connecting the right product or service with the right customer. Offer them a solution to their issue and make it clear to them you are the person to help them solve their issue. Once people develop this trust with you through your messaging, you become the expert.

They will become loyal followers and fans. They will become your best supporters and will share your information and tell everyone about you. They will even come to you asking for help in other areas and will want you to solve ALL of their problems.

Capture Phase Action Exercise:

Summarize what you've just learned from the prior phases to help move to the next phase.

What is your core product or service?

What external problem is your audience facing?

What are the internal fears, doubts, conversations taking place in their heads? Where is your audience now and where do they want to go?

Will your audience pay to have their issues solved by your service/product?

Are you speaking the right messages to your audience?

Are you attracting the right audience or repelling your audience?

What hook can you offer them to provide value?

Phase Four: Convert

The Convert Phase is just as it sounds: Communicate and Convert.

    The Convert Phase is the phase where you will place offers in front of your audience. The offers will be relevant to their issues and will provide the solution, or at least part of the solution, for them to reduce the internal problems and challenges they are facing. You will guide them from an interested audience member to a paying customer.

PAYING customer is the key here. Perhaps your first goal is to gain an extra 2,000 followers, but ultimately getting a sale is where you are leading the customer. This could take time. Some subscribers will follow you for years before converting to a paid customer. If you keep engaging and capturing them while providing value, they will either eventually convert to a paying customer, or recommend/share/promote you so other people do convert to paying customers.

In the digital marketing world, there is a whole dictionary devoted to tactics that are dedicated to helping you convert customers. You've undoubtedly been caught in these tactics as well. I don't mean it as a bad thing. After all, most of it works: UpSells, Down Sells, Cross-sells, One Time Offers, etc.

The details of each conversion funnel tactic are covered in a further advanced Attraction and Conversion Course we offer, but the reason I am bringing them up now is because you don't rely on 'conversion tactics'. Instead, rely on the relationship.

The main thing to understand now about the Conversion Phase is that how you convert them depends on your offer. My overall philosophy on all marketing is:

Be Authentic
Be Present
Give Value

Those who are attracted to your core message will remain loyal and convert. This does not imply a passive approach at all. In fact, it's a very deliberate approach to ensure your target audience knows you are the authority on this topic. You care about them. You and your product are the real deal. All the groundwork we did in the first few phases in understanding your market is what is going to significantly help you in the Conversion Phase.

Remember when I said the work will pay off? It pays off in the Conversion Phase. Why? Because you cared enough in the beginning to understand the problem, the customer, and to position yourself as the expert to really help them.

When you are first dating someone, the fastest way to lose their attention and ensure you don't get a second or third date is to spend all your time talking about yourself. Think about the last person you met who constantly talked about themselves. We all know those people, right? We lose focus fast because we don't think they care. We actually end up thinking of them in a negative way. If you spend those first few dates asking questions, listening, showing up, and being fully engaged and present, you will learn so much about that new person whom you are trying to impress and get to know. They will likely be impressed if you just listen. Why? Because you are showing genuine interest in them and they will feel like you care.

The Formula: Phase Four

People will forget what you said. People will forget what you did. But, people will never forget how you made them feel.
~ Maya Angelou

When you are focused on someone else or your audience, you create a loyal tribe. That should really be the goal: for them to know you care and are genuinely there to help them. Once you achieve this, the Conversion Phase becomes all that much easier, no matter what the product or service may be. There is always value to find.

Now position the offer to convert to a sale.

When you are offering something for your audience to purchase, you must make sure your offer and calls to action are compelling enough for them to jump up wherever they are and say, "Absolutely, Yes!" You've been establishing this along the way with your consistent messaging and follow up with your audience. At this stage, you aren't looking for a "Uh, Sure" or a "Maybe" from your audience. You want the 100%, without a doubt, "Yes! Yes! Oh, Yes! This is for Me, Yes!"

This leads us back to messaging, again. All the work you did in the first three phases continues here with the messaging. Your conversion messages (offers) will be centered around the solutions and how much better their lives will be once they have experienced your product, solution, service, or offer. When you present the offer to them, you will set the stage by painting the picture of how your audience member will think, feel, and react once they have achieved the goal and how their life will be after they implement the solution. You HAVE to connect to them here. You must show them all the solutions. You must show them the state of mind. You are showing them why they should take your offer and how much better they will feel. How it will solve the problem. How it will move them from a state of unhappiness and discontentment to happy and fulfilled. You will paint the picture in the offer showing them what life will be like on the other side. You are showing them all the people who have already experienced the offer/solution and how much better and happier their lives are. Below are a few small examples of some offer statements to help convert:

- By following the Six Simple Steps to Digital Marketing Success, your business will experience exponential growth, leaving you with more time, money, and freedom, enjoying yourself and your business while you attract and engage the right customers who become loyal fans who buy your stuff.
- Marketing will finally feel less overwhelming, less stressful, more fun, simpler, easier, and more enjoyable.
- You won't be able to wait to start a new product or solution and get your offer in front of your audience because it is laid out for you in an easy to follow process.
- Think of how much less stress you will feel knowing that at any time you will be able to attract the perfect customer to you with ease and fun.
- Your customers will be lined up at your door wanting your product or offer. You will finally begin to feel like you are making progress in your business, knowing that you are connecting your message and product with people who get it and want it.

- ➢ You followed a formula that is repeatable and doable in your business at anytime. Your processes are now clear with strategies to grow and continue to explore your business into new levels of success.
- ➢ You can finally cut through all the noise in the confusing marketing world and have confidence knowing that your marketing plan is paying off for you and your business, freeing you from the shackles of being overwhelmed so you can have the fun and freedom you deserve as a hard working business owner. You are now less stressed, more certain about moving forward and overall, more fulfilled.
- ➢ You now go to bed smiling because your business is on autopilot and the hard work has finally paid off.
- ➢ You are now experiencing the lifestyle and business you've always dreamed of because you did the work. YOU made this happen for your business. Your processes are now clear with strategies to grow your business into new levels of success.

- Are you ready TODAY? Are you ready to get into the flow with your audience, simplify your marketing, and have a strategy once and for all that will not only work for you, but also take you further than you've ever imagined?
- Are you ready TODAY to finally have the business and life of your dreams? Are you ready to do the work and feel so proud that you hung in there long enough to see this thing through? You'll finally cut through all the noise and confusion and make sense of all of this for you and your business?
- Are you ready? Let's go….

CALL TO ACTION

All the messaging above and the messaging included in your offer will ask potential customers for a call to action. Purchase now. Apply today. Get yours now. Want to know more? How do I sign up? Join here.

Your call to action has to compel them. It meets them where they are and gets them to take action to move them to where or what they want to experience through the message and offer you are creating for them. They need to raise their hands to say yes and ask how do they buy.

Convert Phase Action Exercise:

Take some time and write all the solutions you are offering.

How will your customers' lives be different by using your product or service?

What experience will they have afterwards, and how much better will their lives become?

The Formula: Phase Four

What will they be missing if they don't experience your offer?

What are some of the offer messages you can present to your audience that will get them to raise their hands and say yes? (Statements that will paint a picture)

What types of calls to action can you create?

Phase Five: Retain

Have you ever been a member of an organization where you completely felt alone, even though the organization was huge? The organization basically forgot about you and you didn't feel a part of it at all. This happens all the time. I know I've felt this way before and it's not fun. In fact, it feels very lonely.

On the flip side, what about experiences where you were part of a group, club, or organization and you felt so welcomed and comfortable, as if you knew everyone and were really part of something where you feel like you belong and are cared for? Which experience is better? This is what we want to keep in mind in the Repeat Phase: how our customers are feeling.

Once you have your followers and have converted them to customers, now you must keep them.

You've done the work to earn their trust, now you have to enter the next phase of the relationship and keep their trust. I suppose each phase we could say is the most critical phase, but retention is one of the most overlooked phases and arguably one of the most important. (I'm pretty sure I've said that at each phase!)

Here is what is interesting about retention. Most people really overlook their clients. I realize in the internet marketing world there are a ton of options and tactics that can be used to get traffic. However, what about the people who have already raised their hands once to say yes and buy from you? Don't those people matter? I'm always amazed at the businesses that get a customer and then toss them aside as if they were yesterday's news. Of course someone is not going to turn around and purchase from you immediately, but they are a HUGE part of your future success.

Let's look at some real data for a moment.

The average conversion rate for a first time visitor to a website is 1-3%. This does not take into account a long time follower. However, once you have converted someone to a customer and they have purchased from you once, you have a 27% higher conversion rate for current customers when they visit your website. Which market would you rather focus on? Traffic that you've not established a relationship with yet and with which you are still building trust, or someone who has said yes already?

To me, this is a no-brainer, and sadly, MOST BUSINESSES GET THIS WRONG.

Instead of focusing on current customers, businesses are constantly looking for new customers. I agree that new customers are important, but don't forget the people who have shown up, said yes, already raised their hands once, and are prime customers. Just like in dating or any relationship, you have to do the work one way or another to continue to build and work to progress the relationship. Perhaps it's worth your time to improve and build upon the relationships you already have rather than starting all over from scratch with new relationships.

The retention phase is VERY overlooked. Once someone has purchased from you, treat him as a VIP. Think about the merchants from whom you purchase and then they add you to a VIP discount list. It creates customer loyalty. Think about the pre-sale events, the current customer events, the loyalty discount cards, the 'members only' clubs. You are more likely to have your loyal clients talk about you and share you with their friends, because they know you and trust you.

- Hold special members-only events
- Special talks
- Special offers and discounts
- Giveaways for members only.

Get creative. Don't just give away tangible gifts, but content: valuable content and additional ways to change their lives and solve their issues. Make sure it's constant value that is above and beyond what you are giving the rest of the market. You may say that you are already giving away so much that how can you possibly do more for your members and paying customers. Well, ask them.

Ask them what is working and what isn't. Answer their questions, be their mentor and guide them. Be consistent. Show up, just as it was in the initial dating phase where you must focus your efforts on listening to the person to learn about them. Now that you're in a relationship doesn't mean you get to flake. You'll get more of a pass for flaking, but you must still show up. Show your commitment. Keep listening, keep engaged, keep coming up with ways to surprise, attract, and grow.

Make sure you categorize your lists and know who has purchased from you so you can treat them like royalty. The more important and special a customer feels, the more likely they are to buy from you again and also talk about you to their friends, i.e., people just like them. Ask them to help you. Make it worth their while to share and talk about you. Help them help you. Create such a VIP treatment that they never want to leave and they want to bring all of their friends with them. Businesses lose creativity in this process and forget that there needs to be a separate plan for the 'already purchased' VIP group.

Regardless of what type of business you have, if you have had people purchase from you in the past, there is a way to make them feel unique and create a deeper more meaningful relationship. Your goal in the retention phase is to build an unbreakable tribe.

Retention Phase Action Exercise:

What questions can you answer for your clients?

What problems are they encountering that may be different once they purchase from you?

What additional fears, doubts, frustrations, pains, desires, wants, and needs do they have?

What retention strategies can you put in place?

In what ways can you show up to continue to commit to and impress your clients?

What three easy strategies can you implement immediately that will treat your clients as VIP's?

Phase Six: Repeat

Once you have really narrowed down your messaging, attracted the perfect prospects, engaged with them, captured their information, converted them into paying customers and created a retention plan, now you get to perfect the process and repeat the cycle.

Just as in prior phases, it's important to do some work and reflection now before you jump into repeating too quickly. You can't change what you don't measure. I use this philosophy in regards to staying in shape. I don't believe in using the scale as a tool for measuring whether I'm in better shape or not.

I use measurements. I record my body measurements, how I feel, and how my energy levels are. These are the measurements I record, then review and reflect every 6-8 weeks if these measurements are changing, or not, and then readjust.

The Repeat Phase is about stepping back, asking questions, and finding out what worked and didn't work, then repeating the process.

In my former career, when I was an accountant for corporations, I was involved in all the nitty-gritty details of measurements, performance, returns, etc. When I left the corporate world to finally pursue my own endeavors, I thought the days of detailed analysis were over. What I learned the hard way was that the nitty-gritty details are essential to growing efficiently. The Repeat Phase is the phase where it's hugely important to get technical and do some number crunching. This is the time to do a thorough analysis of your business. In some instances, this is the phase where you may actually want to start. If you've been in business a while, you can start here to get a good handle on where you currently are and what is working well for you. This will be where you will want to do some re-planning, reprocessing, and yes, repeating. This is where you should take an opportunity to understand and review the important data.

Have you created a system yet where you measure all the important data, or created a dashboard? Just as when you drive a car, boat, or fly a plane, you rely on the instruments to help you gauge whether or not you are on the right course or operating efficiently. Now is the time to create a review process or a dashboard if you don't already have one.

What are the key things to measure and review?

There are many different and important factors when creating your measurement dashboard, but on the following pages are the main acronyms and marketing measurements to learn.

The Digital Marketing Success Formula

CTR — CLICK THROUGH RATE

CTR is the percentage of people who interact.

Are people clicking on your stuff? A high click through rate means a lot of people are interacting with your stuff. This could be via email, ads, facebook posts, download pdfs, videos, offers, ebooks, etc.

ROI — Return On Investment

ROI is usually expressed as a percentage and is to compare a company's profitability or to compare the efficiency of spending efforts. The return on investment formula is: ROI = (Net Profit / Cost of Investment) x 100.

In plain English: Are you making more than you are spending. Are your promotions, efforts, campaigns and decisions bringing in more than you are spending.

CPA — COST PER ACQUISITION

The cost per acquisition is simply how much does it cost you to get a sale or acquire a paying customer.
If you spend $200 on advertising and are selling a $20 ebook, you must convert and obtain 10 paying customers with a CPA less than $20 to be profitable.
Simply stated: How much are you spending for a customer.

The Digital Marketing Success Formula

IMPORTANT ACRONYMS

PPC — PAY PER CLICK

PPC is more self-apparent:
What are you paying per click? If you advertise, what is the cost each time someone clicks on an ad, video or, page?
The goal is to have a low PPC in order to convert a high percentage of customers. It's all about the return.

CTA — CALL TO ACTION

CTA is behavior you wish your audience to take.

Asks your reader to DO something to get them involved or make a decision. Such as commenting, sharing, and opting-in. Build a relationship, which is the foundation of moving them into a 'going steady' relationship versus just saying hi.
Always have some sort of CTA.

The Digital Marketing Success Formula

IMPORTANT ACRONYMS

KPI
Key Performance Indicator

The effectiveness of your marketing efforts as a whole. The performance of the key areas you are targeting. Google Analytics is the most common tool used to measure and track KPI's. It is simplest to get started using.
It measures things such as bounce rate, engagement, time and pages viewed, visitors, to just name a few.

LTV
LIFE TIME VALUE

LTV is in the advanced stages of your marketing. It's how much a customer is worth to you over time. Customers who are loyal and purchase more than once and upgrade have a high LTV. The higher your LTV, the more the traffic in the market you can obtain, the higher ROI, the more campaigns and strategies you can employ. It all works together here and becomes an important component to making further decisions and growing.

The Formula: Phase Six

Recently I attended a lecture by the former CEO of a very successful corporation who eventually sold his shares to his employees. He was talking about the mission statement he created for the organization. It was not just about his goals, but the overall good of the company and the culture he was creating. I found his talk very refreshing as he shared how rapidly and successfully he grew the company. It was impressive not only to see the rapid growth curve, but it was more impressive to see that the growth he achieved was mainly due to the decisions made on the future goals and mission statements all centering around employee and company culture. His personal mission and whole purpose was to create a legacy where his employees would find enough value and respect within the company to eventually purchase it while carrying on the legacy and traditions to pass from generation to generation. He didn't focus 100% on the numbers and profits, but rather the overall mission behind the numbers.

I've never seen such detailed analysis and dashboards inside of a corporation. Even when I was an accountant for large Fortune 50 companies, I didn't do as much analysis as he did with this company. The reason he created such detailed analysis and dashboards was to better communicate with his team and to know where the whole organization needed to focus and improve.

I share this story with you because he used the dashboards to measure data, but kept his focus on the overall mission statement. No matter what your business is or your business goals, knowing your numbers and what they really mean will help you know where you can improve and focus going forward when you repeat your processes.

How do you really understand your conversions? If you implement the acronyms above and review your numbers, you can determine if you are making a profit. You will determine if your cost of acquisition needs to be adjusted. It will show you if you need to tweak your messages and offers. It will establish baselines and create more specific goals. The dashboard you create will set your next launch or promotion up to succeed infinitely better than the last launch or promotion.

Below is a scenario I've created that will help go through a quick analysis of some of the numbers and how the dashboard will help improve when creating the Repeat Phase. This scenario is purely concerning a monetary goal. It does not take into account the mission statement.

Product Launch Scenario:

My goal is to create $2,000,000 on a product launch in twelve months.

I've already run two launches on the product this past year. Therefore, I am looking to dramatically improve my launch the next year to hit this mark.

- Launch Strategy = Webinar Launch. The customer path will look as follows in order to run a successful launch webinar: I will need traffic, who become registrants, who become attendees, and eventually become customers. I use all the prior strategies in the Attract and Engage processes to Capture on the webinar and then during the webinar Convert into paying customers.
- My prior dashboard analysis results looked as follows:

My prior launch resulted in an earned $100,000 with I EPL = $36.

My product was $199 x3 payments or one payment of $525. For analysis purposes let's say my product cost $597.

I sold 167 products totaling $100,000. (rounded up)

84 sold on my first webinar, I had 840 attendees, 2800 Registrants and 9300 Visitors to my webinar ad/ sales page.

The remaining 84 sales came after the webinar with my follow up sequences.

My next launch I want to increase my EPL and also my overall revenue to $2 Million. I know what I did last time, now I need to improve.

The Formula: Phase Six

I need to work backwards this time to reach my goal of $2 Million. I will raise my price this time to $797.

Based upon my prior launch I know that 30% of Visitors to the sales page register for the webinar.

25% of Registrants attend and 10% will purchase. (Half purchased on the webinar, the other half purchased after the webinar before the product close date)

If I strictly assume that my EPL is $36, I would simply say I need 55,555 registrants, but I want to improve, so this is my target.

I now need 2,509 Sales. ($2M/$797), but only need 1,255 sales on the webinar. Therefore, I need 12,550 Attendees. (1255/.10) and

> 50,200 Registrants (12,550/.25). And Traffic/Visitors 167,333 (50,200/.30) This equates to $39 EPL. (2,000,000/50,200)
>
> This doesn't seem like such an increase, but it's up $3 per lead from $36. With this amount of volume and sales, I will take a $1 EPL increase.

This was a quick example and a rough way of looking at a webinar launch strategy to launch a product. There are many other variables that come into play here, but in the scenario above I am assuming I bought all the traffic and had no organic traffic for this webinar.

The message in this section is to know your numbers. You cannot improve if you don't. You cannot scale if you don't. It may seem a little overwhelming at first, but create a fun exercise out of it. Create a dashboard and a baseline. Even if you don't like numbers, try to see if you can beat an EPL, or conversion.

Know the conversions. Review your offers. Know what messaging is working. Know what messaging is not working. The messaging will be directly tied to the conversions. Go back undercover to further deepen your attraction phrases and messages. Review your tactics and decide how to improve in an area that did not work. Now is the time you can tighten up your processes and then add an additional goal, if all things are running smoothly.

We can't solve problems by using the same kind of thinking we used when we created them.
-Albert Einstein

When I first started and ran my businesses, I was really operating them from a sense of urgency and measuring in a haphazard way. Each month I was stressed and worried about how the monthly results would turn out. I figured if my business bank account had a certain dollar amount in it, then I was hitting my goals. I didn't have any of the goals well defined, other than big monetary goals. The big monetary goals were not enough to move me in the direction I wanted and needed to go. I operated from the 'normal' places we are taught as business owners rather than the real places that matter to substantial and fulfilled growth.

When I started to understand all these pieces is when my business took off. I got in the trenches and knew the details by creating a dashboard. I then created strategies inside of each of these phases and understood my market and my messaging. The dashboard and strategies moved me from a place of uncertainty and stress to confidence, certainty, peace and comfort. My business success was then reflecting the way I felt. It wasn't just that I had the plans in place, but I finally felt certain about my plans and the direction that I was moving in. I knew without a doubt that my business would explode and become the success I had dreamt. And It Did! The big goals came to fruition because I believed they would. Believing wasn't good enough in the beginning. I had to act on my belief. When I finally connected all these pieces together, the magic started happening.

The Formula: Phase Six

This is my wish for you also: to make the magic happen. And the good news is YOU can do it, with less stress than I ever did.

Repeat Phase Action Exercise:

Take some deep reflection time based upon your results and study the following:

What messaging worked? What didn't?

What types of people did you attract, and were they the right fit?

Do you need to tweak the audience? How can you change your messaging to attract a different audience?

Did you engage with them? How? Are you focused on the right engagement strategy?

Were you responsive? Did you address their needs, or yours?

Did they respond to what you were giving them? Was it valuable?

Did you capture? How?

Did you create a clear Call To Action?

Did you ask them to share? Were they responsive? Did you create incentive to share?

Did you create loyalty and offers that your audience couldn't refuse to share?

What are your numbers?

Did you create a dashboard?

What is on your dashboard?

Do you know your customer LTV?

Did you have a promotion?

Do you know your EPL?

What is your CTR on offers?

Once you can answer some of these questions, you can adjust your strategies, your messages and re-launch, then repeat. Reflect and review, then repeat again.

The Formula: Phase Six

DAILY REMINDER:

THE BEST WAY TO GET SOMETHING DONE IS TO BEGIN

www.heatherjcrider.com

Where To Start

Now that we've gone through the phases in more detail, the natural questions are "Where to Start?" or "Where to Improve?" Where do you implement all these phases and let these juicy, creative offers flow from you to your customers? Most people want to jump straight into creating or selling. If we go back and look at each of the phases, the most important thing is to take time to research and plan.

As I've said before, one of the most important parts to success is planning and creating a well-defined strategy. This guide isn't intended to review all of the different tools that you can use to implement your strategies. Tools change. Tools come and go. Tools aren't as important as we like to make them. If the strategies aren't in place, you can't effectively communicate to the right audience.

I remember years ago that when I was trying to grow my practice, I purchased ALL the tools I could think of. I spent a great deal of time mastering the intricacies and details of each of the tools. They are important to helping you grow your business, but not if you jump the gun. This is what I have done, more than once. I was so eager to grow that I thought if I had the latest and greatest tools and tricks it would help me. It did help, but only marginally. I could deliver a few things more efficiently, but it wasn't until I really took a few giant steps backwards and reflected on the real steps I needed to take to grow. I then created the phases and processes we already described earlier in this book. In order for me and my business to grow, I had to understand the phases in more detail.

I needed a real strategy, not just a monetary goal.

This was probably the biggest lesson my businesses taught me. My intentions and heart have always been in the right place, but it wasn't until I connected my brain to my heart and created detailed strategies, messages, and deliverables, that my business finally started to grow. The growth that not only I've achieved, but also the businesses that I've helped along the way, have all been a direct result of the phases and strategies discussed above.

Everyone, including me, has wanted a secret or a shortcut to having a successful business. After years of spinning my wheels and making costly errors, I realized the biggest shortcut was to research and master the needs of your market as well as mastering these phases. The real goal is to implement one or two marketing strategies that will make a big impact on your business. Honestly, the technical tools change so rapidly that it's almost impossible to narrow down the exact tools and tactics that will work for you. But, I'm here to help!

MARKETING METHODS

YES. Finally. We get all this foundation stuff out of the way.

Well, don't get too excited just yet. Before we talk about the tactical implementation, make certain you've done the work in the prior phases. Mainly phases one through four. It's imperative to understand your market to properly plan your conversion strategy. You may be able to sell snow to an Eskimo, but if they don't need it, they won't come back for more or become a loyal customer of yours. Just as we talked about your overall goals, it's important to have ONE or, at most, two marketing methods.

When looking at each marketing method, it's important to understand that comparing the methods is kind of like comparing the fruit in a fruit salad. It's all fruit, but each one has its own unique flavor, texture, quality, and benefits.

Choose one or two methods to implement. Test the method. Dedicate some time to making it work for you. Far too often I see business owners who try a marketing method and then get frustrated and quit too early. Not all methods work for all businesses. But NO method will work if you don't give it a fair shot. Marketing is all about testing. I can give you a blueprint that will lessen your learning curve. If you follow it, it will work. But along the way, you will need to test, tweak, test, and tweak again, because each market is different. This is how marketing works. Things are changing daily. Your audience shows up in different ways, on different days. You must test. I hope I have made this clear: you must be patient, and test.

Email Marketing

Email works! It's The #1 Method. End of Story.

So many marketers feel email marketing is an antiquated method of communicating with your audience. They are very wrong. It works, and works well.

Have you ever heard the phrase "Build A List", or "The Money Is In Your List?"

Building an email list is the number one way to grow your business.

In your email marketing you will create different stages, phases, and strategies. It's a strategy inside of a strategy. There is a process of collecting email addresses, sending targeted emails to your list to keep them interested, targeted engagement, offers to provide value, free stuff, offers to buy stuff, advice, cool stuff to entertain and share, more value in the form of offers, and feel good stuff.

Do you see the success phases in that process? When you are ready to grow and even explode, having specific email marketing strategies will help you. In our advanced marketing growth courses, we go over this in much more detail. Until you are ready for the advanced methods, just keep in mind the success phases when you are developing your email or newsletters.

Email has been around a long time now, some 42 years. I recently wrote a blog post about how important it is to get rid of the noise and distractions our email inboxes sometimes create. Today, my inbox has over 14,000 email messages. Now, to be fair, I have a lot of email accounts and manage quite a few clients' accounts as well. Not all of those messages are unnecessary. But, the point remains that we can sometimes get too many emails.

Don't let this deter you, however. I'm only saying as marketers and entrepreneurs we are bombarded by new sales tools, software, programs, etc. Unless those things serve us 100% at the moment, we should unsubscribe to help us manage the overwhelming number of emails.

Most people are caught up with their social media followers. This can be important later in further marketing strategies and branding, and with capturing new audiences. But the reason people are caught up with the number of followers they have is because of the visible reaction. The number of followers we have satisfies our need for immediate gratification and celebrity. This is all great, but you don't own your social media followers (we will talk about this more later). You do, however, own your email list.

There are too many studies on the effectiveness of email marketing to list. But here are a few notable studies to point out:

In 2016, Adestra performed a study that indicated of the participants surveyed, nearly 68% of teens, and 73% of millennials said they prefer to receive communication from a business via email. Also, more than 50% rely on email to buy things online.

60% of Internet marketers polled believe email marketing outperforms social media. Email gets more immediate exposure to your subscribers.

In other words, if you have 2,000 email subscribers, 2,000 Facebook fans and 2,000 followers on Twitter – with the average open rates polled (22%) and the average reach and CTR (6% Facebook and 2% Twitter):

435 people will open your email.

120 Facebook fans will see your message.

40 Twitter followers will see your message.

Small business trends show that the benefits of email are substantial and striking, especially compared to social and search channels. It's estimated that you get a $39.40 return on every $1 invested into email marketing. I don't know how you feel about returns, but that's a pretty good return on investment in my book.

If I made any mistake when I co-founded my first Internet marketing company, it was not actively employing dedicated campaigns for email marketing. Instead, I focused on client attraction and service campaigns (see the top three marketing mistakes.). These were all great things to grow a business, but it did not sustain long-term relationships. It was much more transactional, perhaps more of the traditional way of thinking. And it was much more in alignment with how we were taught, but it didn't really scale in a long term way.

Email is still the #1 most effective marketing tool. Remember when it was a big deal to receive newsletters from your favorite store or author? It was full of goodies, the latest and greatest and hidden offers. Then everyone started sending out newsletters.

In terms of email marketing and growing your list, do you think newsletters are considered email? Yes and No. Reconsider an e-newsletter, unless it packs a punch. Static Newsletters aren't enough. The goal of email is to continue the Success Formula. Attract, Engage, Capture, Convert, and Retain. Your email or newsletters should always include some of these success elements and be kept clear.

Always keep your messaging clear and include the elements that are found in the phases. Know the goal of the message. Have actions and topics that are in direct relationship to the audience. Include the key phrases that you've been working on.

Now I get to say, "I told ya so!" (but I mean it in the most loving way possible). I want you to succeed, which is why I am a stickler for the foundational groundwork and strategy work we did in the first five phases. The messaging is the key. Yes, I've said that already, and I'll keep saying it, too.

Keep your messages relevant and about your audience. Anyone can email, post on social media, purchase a domain and 'start a company.' The magic is in your messaging and in you. Make it worth your audience's time to engage with you. Always incorporate those key phrases in your email. Create catchy, attractive phrases to grab the attention of your audience from the research you did on your audience concerning their issues, wishes, fears, goals, etc. All of these phrases are solid gold for you. Always include them in your marketing messaging whether it is email or not.

Your goal in all phases is to create loyalty and trust in order to convert people into loyal paying customers.

You will want to test your email constantly, but always remain consistent with communication. Make sure to create an environment with your emails that excites your customers and causes them to open your emails. Be different here, and always give value. Offer ways for your customers to interact with you. If your message and offers resonate with your audience, you will keep your audience and will be more effective with email.

We will talk more about how to grow your email list in a few pages when we talk about tactical traffic sources. For now, once you have emails, stay the course. They work.

Methods Action Exercise:

What are some of the best email messages you have received?

What are some of the best subject lines you have received?

Create a few catchy email subject lines here for practice.

Content Marketing

Content is King.

What does that mean? It's what you create and share. It's the good stuff that creates value and turns your readers/audience/listeners into paying

customers who will remain paying customers. It's what excites them and causes them to want more. It's the stuff that allows them to understand you and your business better. It's the stuff that they can't wait to talk about and share with others. It's the good stuff you create to share information and ideas, that eventually leads to the sale of a product or service.

Think about people you may know: Tim Ferriss, Michael Hyatt, John Maxwell, Tony Robbins, Brendan Burchard, or any of the other big names. What they all have in common is consistent content that's high quality and leaves you wanting more. It transforms you in some ways because they set themselves up as the expert in their areas. You don't have to be a big name to have powerful and meaningful content. You don't have to be an Internet marketer to have powerful content. You just have to create it and share it. No matter what your business or end goal, providing great content and transformational information will create a loyal customer base.

Think about someone or a company that sent you information (content) that you found incredibly valuable. Even if it didn't directly relate to them, but rather something that was useful to you. What was it? Was it an eBook? A course? A video? A series of videos? Multiple messages? A webinar? A link? Why was it valuable to you? How did it help you?

Did you comment on it? Did you share it? Did you talk about it? What would make you share it? What are the things that really mean something to you? Some of the most shared content is shared because it was of huge value to its recipients.

I just went through a video series from a friend of mine whom I've known for several years. He always over-delivers on his content. This video series, that was all free, gave me so many new lessons and perspectives I had not thought of. Plus, it was entertaining and kept me engaged far longer than I expected it to. Even if I knew some of the content or strategies inside of it, his perspective was good to hear and see. These lessons were so valuable that I was willing to share them. And, you know what: so were thousands of other people.

Quality Content Gets Shared.

That's why having good content is important. Good content never dies. Good content will go viral. Good content gets talked about. Good content is magical. Good content let's your audience work for you.

Methods

Let's face it: there are thousands of courses, companies, and trainings available. You may be thinking that it's all been done before. However, there is ONLY ONE YOU! Your content is unique. Get your content out there. You have something to say.

What is your product or service? How will it solve your audience's issues? Talk about how it will solve the issue. Talk about one simple way your product or service will make their lives better. Perhaps you can show them demonstrations. Content is anything that will create value.

What types of things would interest your audience, even if it's not 100% related to your product or service? Is it valuable for your audience? If so, then you should create and share.

You may be thinking, "But, I can't give away all my stuff for free." Most people feel they have to immediately sell something. I get this struggle, especially if you are just starting out and 'need' a sale. Giving some content away for free doesn't mean you have nothing left to offer. Of course, if your business is physical merchandise (e.g. a clothing line or furniture), you cannot give your entire inventory away (unless you really want to make some headlines!) But, you still have something to offer that will provide some benefit without getting a sale first.

We will talk in future lessons about strategies to help you create a patch or bridge in your business to create immediate income. The goal right now is to understand content. Once someone connects with you and your content, you've created an unshakable bond. Take time and deliberate effort when you release any content.

Just as we spent a considerable amount of time researching your audience for messaging, take some time before you release content and really be thorough and complete. Put all you have into it. If you just release something for the sake of releasing it, chances are it won't resonate with your audience. Take time and over deliver on something that is valuable. This is how you get noticed and create attractive content. Great content gets shared. It gets interaction. It gets engagement.

The Digital Marketing Success Formula

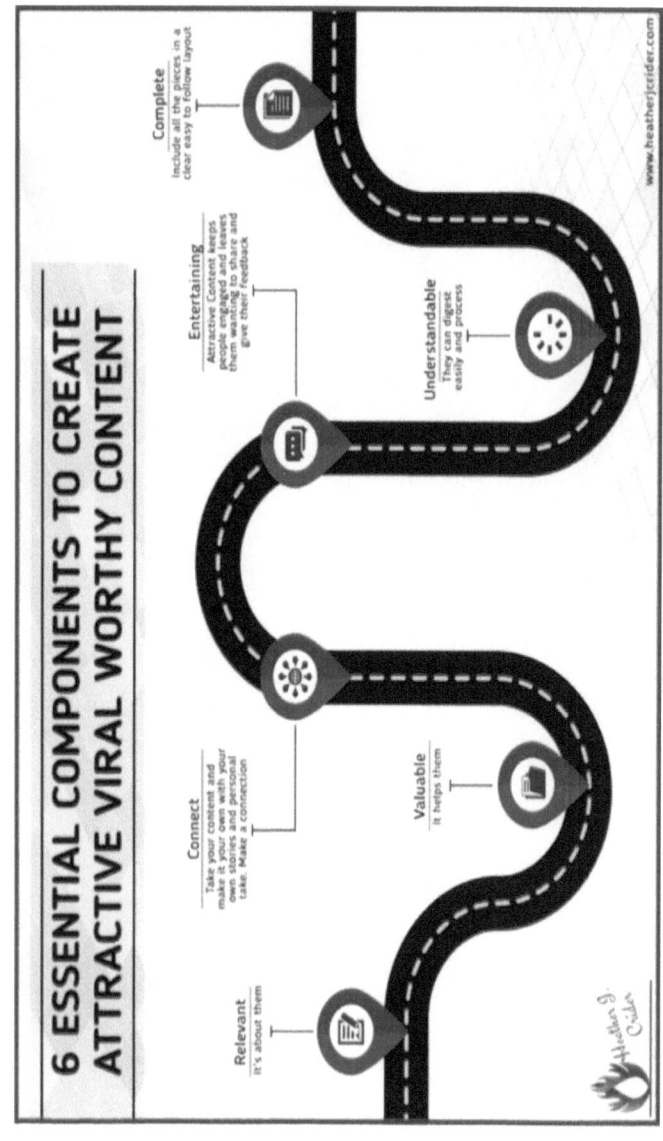

Six Essential Components To Create Attractive Viral-Worthy Content

1. Relevant

    It's about them.

2. Valuable

    It helps them.

3. Understandable

    They can digest it easily and process.

4. Connect

    Make it your own with your own stories and personal take.

5. Complete

    Include all the pieces in a clear and simple layout.

6. Entertaining

    Attractive content keeps people engaged and leaves them wanting to share and give their feedback.

NOW YOU CAN CREATE! Go through the Six Essential Components and Get to Creating!

Content Action Exercise:

Do you have an idea brewing and want to share it?

What kinds of content can you create?

What are some messages or videos that will resonate with your audience?

What's your message?

What are the deliverables?

Getting Traffic

Traffic sources tend to be one of the most talked about buzzwords and misunderstood parts of the digital marketing world. What is traffic anyways? It is simply places where your audience hangs out or where you can wave your hand to your audience and say hello. It's not that complicated: just keep getting your message out consistently. That sounds easy, but how?

There are a lot of different types of traffic sources, and when you are reviewing them all you need to go with the ones that work for you. Just as we keep talking about, pick one or two traffic sources, and then add as you go. Mastering all traffic sources is not possible, since it's too complicated to do all at once. Are your clients/audience located at the traffic source? Find out if they are there. In the Attract Phase, we learned to conduct research to discover the spots where your audience hangs out. Pick one or two places they are hanging out and deliver your message. Keep it simple. Don't overcomplicate it, and stay consistent.

Remember the details of the six phases we covered and implement the strategies of the phases when you pick your traffic methods.

Attract/Engage/Capture/Convert/Retain/Repeat.

Types of Traffic Sources

Email Marketing and Content Marketing are the main marketing campaigns to employ.

Traffic Sources to gain exposure include:
- Social Media
- Blogs
- Websites
- Guest Blogs
- Featured Articles/Publications
- Press Releases
- Live Streams

- Podcasts
- TV/Video Appearances
- Email Lists
- Guest Email Lists
- Friends & Family Lists
- PPC
- SEO
- Relationships
- Your list - Let it work for you

That's a lot, but that's why gaining traffic and getting yourself in front of traffic should be a step-by-step approach. One step at a time. If you attempt to use all traffic sources at once, none will work. It will overwhelm you if you employ them all at the same time.

In our masterminds and advanced mastery courses, we really do a deep dive into all the traffic methods to tie it all together and create a fully functional, well-oiled machine and funnel. However, you don't need a complicated funnel for things to work. You can always add layers to your strategies, but remember to add layers slowly. People usually get so focused on traffic that they can easily lose the forest for the trees.

Create a weekly or monthly calendar. I suggest for my clients and students to pick a content theme each week, or even each month. Then each post/conversation/article/content offering will be around that theme. If you write a blog, post that blog article on your social media platform. If you podcast, talk about the blog, or vice versa. Email your list the blog, or a partial intro to the blog and a link back to the blog so they can visit it directly. Provide an incentive to do it, such as a teaser, or a question. The formula for traffic is simply to make a decision each month and stick to the plan. When you release content, do so with a follow up plan.

Traffic is all about your strategy. This goes back to the earlier question, "What is your goal?" If you are trying to gain followers, then perhaps a social media and PPC strategy will gain followers whom you can begin to attract and engage. Then you will lure them to your email list by the 'hook' created in the Capture Phase. Then, once in your email list, you will repeat Phases 1-3 a few times before moving to Phase

Four and offering your product or service that will Convert. Do you see how the Phases will always play into your strategy?

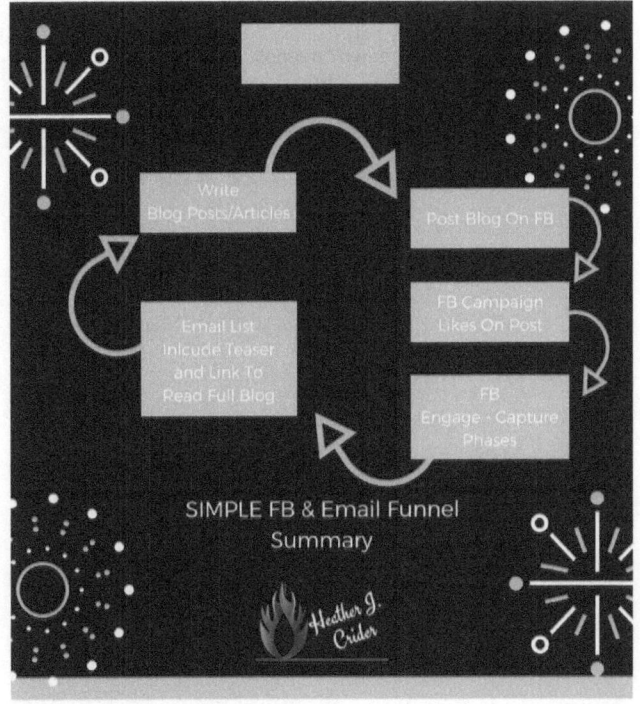

Social Media

Finally, we get to talk about social media. This is a big one! Social media is everywhere. I marvel each day at all the new social media platforms being formed, all the while learning of the numerous ones I never even heard of. We could spend days talking about social media: the good, the bad, and the ugly. My goal is to keep it simple and lay out the facts.

First of all, you need a plan. I know it's tedious, but it's SO worth it, especially with social media. Initially, you have to understand that with social media there is no secret sauce, magical fairy dust, or quick-fix button. It just doesn't happen like that. I'm pretty sure every marketer has attempted to uncover the secret sauce, and the truth is that there isn't one. Social media is ever-changing, and the best thing to do is to create a plan that works for you. Test, tweak, re-test, and re-tweak. It will be ever changing, but with a solid plan, you'll make significant progress toward your goals.

Have you ever logged on to Facebook, scrolled for a few minutes, and then realized it's been a few hours? I'm guilty of that myself.

Social media is the ultimate time vampire.

When Pinterest first came out, I almost went bankrupt because of all the time I spent finding ideas, and interesting things. It was so distracting that I had to make a promise to work for so many hours each day before I could even pick up Pinterest. I've calmed down now after some intense Pinterest self-talks. Social media can swallow you, just as it can swallow your audience.

Social media is a great way to engage and build an audience, but a lot of business owners have false expectations when they are first attempting to gather a following. Business owners, entrepreneurs, and marketers want the quick fix. They feel that with one or two posts they will have a viral affect and become an overnight sensation. It can perhaps happen, but just like winning the lottery, the odds are not in your favor.

Why is the social media marketing strategy not the number one strategy to start off your marketing? Here are a few reasons:

As mentioned above, it's a time vampire. When you are scrolling through any social media platform, think about how quickly you view it. Most people race through. What catches your attention? Standing out in a crowded room can sometimes be a challenge. It's not a guarantee you will. It takes patience and devotion. Social media should always be a secondary or supplementary strategy, not a first one.

If all of your followers are on Instagram, what happens if Instagram gets shut down or stops working? How will your followers find you? What if a social media platform changes the way you engage and present to your followers? Have you ever heard of paying to boost your post to your own followers? I'm not singling anyone out here or anything, but Facebook has changed their policies to force your hand concerning advertising and boosting to your own audience. Stated another way: you don't own your followers on social media.

How many different social media platforms are there? There are too many to choose, and not only can it be a time vampire for you, but it can also consume your entire strategy. Each platform has its own intricacies and quirks. So pick one, maybe two, at most.

Winning with Social Media

Social media is a good idea. Don't let anything I just said deter you from using social media. As long as the right plan is put in place at the right time. Although social media is a time vampire and can be complex, don't let it get you down. You've come this far and have worked so hard already. Just add another channel to distribute your content. ***You should think of social media as a distribution channel for your content.***

Traffic Through Social Media

There should always be strategies in place to implement social media content and obtain traffic.

Remember all the content you created when you mastered the 'Content is King' concept? Now is the time to use it.

Take one article you've written or video you've made and slice it into different pieces. As I stated earlier, I suggest themes. Perhaps your business is a physical product. For one whole week maybe your theme is centered around accessories. This is where a little pre-planning comes into place. Do you also sell any accessories? If so, great. You can create videos or ebooks on the accessories. Each day you can schedule the release of the videos or books. Ask your followers to share the video. Have a contest that whoever shares it with or tags three people will be entered into a drawing for free merchandise.

This is the fun part. If you have a theme each month or day of the week, you can stay much more engaged and consistent, and see how people are reacting to you. You can even record yourself live while answering questions, and then post it on your secondary social media channel. Expand on your amazing content and make sure people understand it in all formats. Reformat it, so people will consume it in the various methods.

Ways you can reformat your methods include:
- ❖ Infographics
- ❖ Videos and Video Series

- ❖ Break an original video up into smaller pieces
- ❖ Transcribe your video into a .pdf and redistribute in print
- ❖ Create short e-books with the content
- ❖ Host Facebook lives or various live streams
- ❖ Exclusive webinars
- ❖ Special Tele-seminars
- ❖ Become a featured guest on podcast
- ❖ Become a featured blog guest

Schedule

Create a posting schedule. It's important to have a posting schedule to help you save time and become more efficient. My suggestion for clients, and what I implement for them, is a monthly posting calendar. This is such an efficient way to manage your content. You can always change along the way, but you will then understand and have a better sense of how to manage. When you pick your theme, you can then outline where you will post, when, and how.

Perhaps you write one main article for the month, then all your content is reformatted and released from the topics of that main article. Having the schedule and some automation will help you become more efficient.

Know when to post.

Just as you should create your own posting schedule, also find out when the optimal posting time is for each social media platform. The algorithms are always changing, so the optimal posting times will likely adjust every so often. We can discuss this in more detail in future seminars and videos.

The Digital Marketing Success Formula

VISUAL MARKETING STRATEGY

Discover why you need a better visual content strategy to get noticed

As social media has gained momentum and users, so has the impact of visual content. Every major social network, including Facebook, Twitter, Instagram and Pinterest have had updates.

Users are becoming more savvy with their social media use making the need for video and infographics a more effective way to communicate with readers.

SOCIAL MEDIA STATS

 Tweets with images received 150% more retweets than tweets without images

 On Instagram, photos showing faces get 38% more Likes than photos not showing faces

 Facebook posts with images see 2.3X more engagement than those without images.

52% of teens use Instagram, and nearly as many (41%) use Snapchat.

46 PERCENT
of marketers say photography is critical to their marketing and storytelling strategies

34 PERCENT
of marketers selected visual assets as their most important content

73 PERCENT
of content creators plan to prioritize creating more content in 2016

http://www.heatherjcrider.com

Automate

This is really a huge time saver. Once you've created your content and created a schedule of when to post it, now use an automatic scheduler to post your content for you. This helps at the beginning of the month or the beginning of each week. Schedule the content and have the automatic scheduler post it for you. A lot of the following platforms will let you manage and engage with your audience directly from the platform as well.

Social Media Automation Tools
-Buffer
-Meet Edgar
-Hootsuite
-CoSchedule
-HeatherJCrider Social Media: This is my own branded social media scheduler. It's an easy to use and free tool with editing features. If you would like a free account you can signup at
www.social.heatherjcrider.com/signup

How do you get more traffic through social media? ASK!

Your audience will want to help you. Create simple ways for people to share your content. At the end of each email, or some of the most valuable emails, simply add a Twitter or Facebook link. Have it in a quick and easy format ready to go so they can share it. If you have an article or download you want to give them, ask them to share something to get the copy. Create an incentive for your audience to share.

In the example earlier I talked about one company having contests. You can even have contests giving away something that is related to your product, but not the product itself. There are a ton of iPad giveaways and other related ones. These are perhaps a little gimmicky, but if you have a product that you need to get in front of an audience, these types of gimmicks do work. In your main featured posts, ask for reposts. If you have a free course, webinar, video, or seminar your audience will want their friends to join, make it simple for them to share. Offer bonuses and just be creative.

Always Use Visuals.

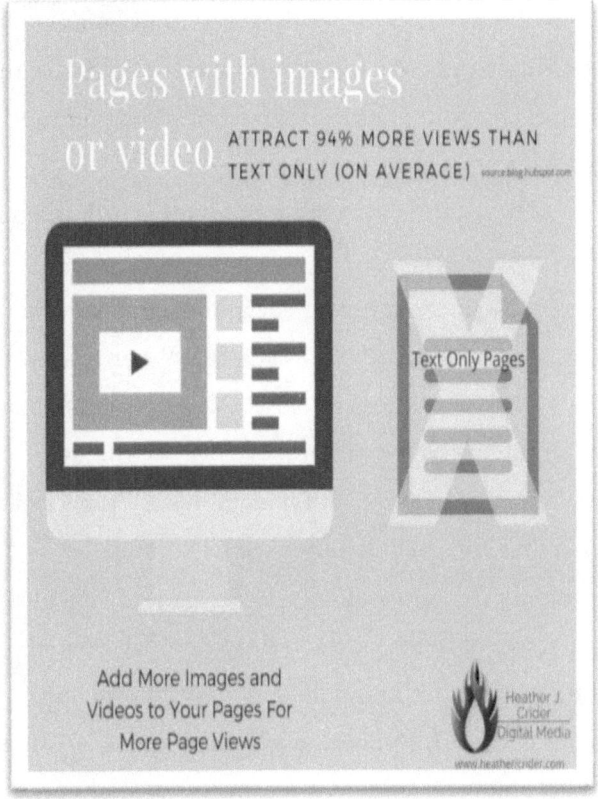

Images are so important to get the attention of your audience, or newcomers.

Video Marketing Strategy

Video Marketing is something that must be talked about. I said earlier that you should master your email and content marketing first. Those are the two best strategies. Video marketing is another tool to distribute your content.

If a picture is worth a thousand words, then a video is priceless!

Look through your social media newsfeeds and count how many videos you see. When you watch TV, why do commercials exist? We are visual beings, and graphics paint a picture. We can see things thoroughly with video and images. It's the power of video that will grab the attention of potential customers. Websites will get 85-90% more views with some form of image and/or video than with text alone. Images are impactful and very helpful, but videos will hook attention much more quickly. Just as infographics can show you a process, idea, or concept, video achieves this in a far more powerful and effective manner.

Plan your video marketing strategy and have a goal in mind. Are you wanting to gain attention and attraction? Then have a Call to Action in place. Is your video a sales video? Are you wanting your audience to share your video so you can gain more followers?

What types of videos should you use? The short answer is any. In reality, when you implement a video marketing strategy, it will become another marketing arm that you will form and test. You are testing what works with your audience. It will show how much attention, engagement, and conversion you receive. Any video that is produced in a decent manner will gain some attraction and attention. Keep the same Success Formula Phases in mind when you are piecing together a video or having one made for you. It's important to clearly convey your message in the video using the Success Formula.

Types of Videos:
- Voice over text
- Animation
- Whiteboard and Blackboard Doodle Video

- ❖ Commercial-Style Videos showcasing products
- ❖ Instructional Videos teaching and showing off your stuff
- ❖ Live-stream video talking to your audience
- ❖ Videos from your smartphone

You don't need to have an absolutely amazing production to get it in front of your audience. Just get it out there. There is always room to improve quality and integrate gadgets in later advanced phases.

Video should not be used alone, however. Video should be used as a secondary method. It should be a compliment to what you are already doing.

PPC

PPC stands for Pay Per Click. It is simply paid advertising on any of the traffic sources. There are PPC campaigns and strategies for each type of traffic source. Facebook ads are the most common, and if you're going to try any paid traffic advertising, probably the best to start with.

Does it work?

It can, with the right strategy in place, and the right timing. However, pull the reigns back on this one and don't implement traditional PPC too soon. My opinion is that when you are implementing your marketing methods, you should never start with paid advertising. Take the time to create content and master your messaging. Most marketers want to get aggressive and go after paid traffic, and you can, when you're ready.

Really be patient here and take the time to make attractive viral-worthy content well before you spend any money on paid advertising. A lot of businesses are eager to spend $2,000 on a paid ad in hopes of getting $3 for every $1 spent. This can happen, but not at first. There's not enough momentum for it to be worthwhile just yet. You'll need some definitive proof and a library of content first.

In further advanced methods, there are ways of using what's called the Bridge Technique that will help you gain attractive audience members early. Before you can dive into these advanced techniques, you still need attractive viral-worthy content first. People need to see a presence from you and connect with you. Your ROI will thank you for this.

Why is PPC so complicated?

It's because most people throw it out there hoping it sticks, just like they do with all the other methods. The reason I suggest waiting for PPC is that you must know what is working first. All the viral-worthy content, social sharing, email sharing, and email returns are important.

I came from the financial world, so knowing your numbers was required. But, a lot of people don't want to take the time to understand the numbers and metrics of what is working. It can be boring, confusing, and overwhelming to sort out the numbers, but wouldn't you rather know the average open rate, click-through rate, and the number of social shares you are getting? This will help you understand if your content is really resonating. Then, and only then, can you venture out into the depths of PPC. You need to understand your ROI. This is very important before you can truly profit from your investments and really crank it up. Plus, you'll likely get too discouraged if it doesn't work well from the beginning.

It's exciting to see returns. If you put $1 in a vending machine and it spits out $2, wouldn't you stand there and do that all day long? Absolutely! Who wouldn't? It is possible to do this, and PPC will work for you, once you have a solid foundation. Knowing the numbers is essential for growth, and PPC is no exception to this rule. Facebook is a great way to test paid traffic. If you start slowly and really hone in on a small audience, you can test how your content is resonating. Then go through the numbers.

We cover PPC with much greater depth in an advanced course.

The Digital Marketing Success Formula

Advanced Methods

In our Advanced Digital Marketing Mastery Course, we will really roll up our sleeves and do some work with advanced automation strategies. I'll summarize below some of these strategies, but if you would like more detail on this course, just send an email to **admin@heatherjcrider.com**.

SEO

SEO is Search Engine Optimization. It is a highly debated, misleading, and always confusing method. Search engine optimization is the process of ranking your website for the key terms your ideal audience is searching for so you can be placed at the top of the search engine rankings to gain organic traffic.

Make sense? I didn't think so. Simply stated, SEO tries to put your website at the top of Google searches to be seen, organically. It's like standing on top of a table in a crowded room so your audience can find you and see you above everyone else.

I spent a lot of years solely focusing on SEO for clients and ranking hundreds of websites. I'll warn you now: SEO is a long and tedious process. It can pay off significantly with the right formula at the right stages of your business. There are groups and many marketers who focus solely on SEO. The SEO formula is always changing, however, since Google updates their algorithms frequently to ensure the best quality sites are being positioned on the top of page one of searches.

SEO is one of the last strategies to employ because of the long and time-consuming process. SEO is also a long-term investment, meaning you won't see an immediate return on your investment as you may with other methods. If you have a large budget, then by all means implement it sooner rather than later.

SEO can be great, but once people find you, you must convert them. This is why following the Success Formula always works best. Know when to implement the right methods at the right time. SEO is an advanced traffic method. I consider it an advanced method and suggest seeking a digital marketing expert, who thoroughly understands ranking and SEO, to help you rank your website.

There are definitely things you can do along the way to assist with your rankings, and I have a new series coming out soon, which will be a beginner's guide to ranking your website, and converting your traffic. In the meantime, just keep it simple. Basic SEO is making sure your website content, the site title, and page titles are all relevant to the main keywords that your audience/clients are searching.

Funnel Marketing

Funnel Marketing is essentially the stages you move your audience through to convert them into paying customers. It's the Success Formula automated. Funnel Marketing is utilizing the mechanics and the tools to automate and implement the Success Formula.

Search Engine Marketing

Search Engine Marketing is the entire process tied together in a systematic way to achieve all of your goals and create loyal paying customers who talk about you and share your content with others. SEM is the whole pie, not just the pieces.

Slivers

Slivers includes the campaigns and goals inside of each campaign that we have already mentioned.

-Email Marketing
-Content Marketing
-Attraction
-Engagement
-Retention
-Streamlining your website and funnels
-Connecting your website and email lists
-Connecting your website and social media
-Sharing
-Funnels

Advanced Methods

- Offers
- Media
- SEO
- Conversion
- Systematizing to Repeat

Now what?

Any learning curve can be steep, and no matter how long you have had your business, the strategies and formulas discussed here will help you grow and hopefully eliminate further learning curves.

What we've covered in the success formula:

- ✓ What mistakes to avoid
- ✓ The importance of planning in each Phase and method
- ✓ The Digital Marketing Formula
- ✓ How to become a mind reader by researching the biggest issues your audience is facing
- ✓ Narrowing down the one or two goals of YOUR marketing plan
- ✓ Engage your audience by speaking their language and offering value
- ✓ Go where your audience is
- ✓ The magic is in the messaging
- ✓ Convert your audience by creating an "Oh, yes!" offer
- ✓ Create a retention strategy to have a loyal, happy base of repeat-buying customers

Advanced Methods

- ✓ Reflect upon and analyze what works to repeat the process in each marketing method
- ✓ The importance of an email marketing campaign
- ✓ How to create attractive viral-worthy content
- ✓ How to manage and use social media
- ✓ The value of video marketing
- ✓ PPC Overview
- ✓ Grow with the funnel
- ✓ Advanced Techniques and Search Engine Marketing Overview

Now that you know the basics and how to proceed, it's time to practice and grow your business. Is it hard? Yep, it sure is. Nothing worth doing or having is ever easy. The good news is that it will pay off. I have a resource list on my website that lists all the basic tools you can use, and some advanced ones as well.

For now, the goal of this book was to give you a better understanding of your plan, the strategies, and how to actually implement them and interact with potential customers. Business owners and entrepreneurs are often confused by digital marketing, and their time is seemingly wasted mainly because they just want to implement but don't really take the necessary time to develop the strategies and plans that will not only benefit them, but make them more profitable, while doing less.

Wouldn't it be worth your time to do some hard work now in order to work less and have more fun in the future?

Plan ~ Create ~ Implement

About the Author

Heather has been a life long student who took an

interest at an early age in personal development, growth, and entrepreneurship.

She eagerly started her first business ironing clothes at the age of five and then at the age of nine started a flea market store from her shed. These early lessons have carried with her throughout her life.

Heather has founded and grown four successful companies in the financial and marketing industries. She also worked for Fortune 100 companies such as Caterpillar, Inc., and Nestle, in management and accounting.

As part of Heather's passion for growth and development, she has been trained and certified in numerous personal development, leadership, mindfulness, health and transformational programs.

Heather lives near St. Louis and enjoys spending time with her two amazing children, friends, and family. She is a fitness and health advocate and devotes her spare time to increasing the awareness of a successful fulfilled life through food, fitness and sometimes saying "F'IT".

Join Heather's Private Facebook group to learn more strategies to increase your personal and business growth: Extraordinary Fulfillment

https://www.facebook.com/groups/316647125379603/

Drop by and say hi:

www.heatherjcrider.com

https://www.facebook.com/BeyondYourMaximumPotential/

admin@heatherjcrider.com

www.ingramcontent.com/pod-product-compliance
Lightning Source LLC
Chambersburg PA
CBHW031629210526
45464CB00004B/1818